GERMANY

BY RACQUEL FORAN

Essential Library
An Imprint of Abdo Publishing
abdobooks.com

ABDOBOOKS.COM
Published by Abdo Publishing, a division of ABDO, PO Box 398166, Minneapolis, Minnesota 55439.

Printed in the United States of America, North Mankato, Minnesota.
102022
012023

Cover Photo: Sean Pavone/Shutterstock (castle); Shutterstock (pattern)
Interior Photos: Canada Stock/Shutterstock, 4–5, 9, 27; Shutterstock, 7, 12, 18, 24–25, 28–29, 30, 57, 84, 88, 93, 101; Florian Monheim/Bildarchiv Monheim GmbH/Alamy, 10; Iulius Agency/Shutterstock, 14–15; Andrew Mayovskyy/Shutterstock, 16–17; Konrad Kerker/Shutterstock, 19; Kovaleva Ka/Shutterstock, 21; Peter Hermes Furian/Shutterstock, 23 (Germany); Web Tools/Shutterstock, 23 (globe); Gertjan Hooijer/Shutterstock, 31; Sean Gallup/Getty Images News/Getty Images, 33; Christian Peters/Shutterstock, 35; Klaus-Dietmar Gabbert/Picture Alliance/Getty Images, 36–37; Britta Pedersen/Picture Alliance/Getty Images, 38–39; CM Dixon/Print Collector/Hulton Archive/Getty Images, 40; Heritage Images/Hulton Archive/Getty Images, 41; Stefano Zaccaria/Shutterstock, 42; Milos Oberajger/Topical Press Agency/Hulton Archive/Getty Images, 45; Berliner Verlag/Archiv/Picture Alliance/dpa/AP Images, 46–47; Fred Ramage/Keystone Features/Hulton Archive/Getty Images, 49; Fredrik von Erichsen/Picture Alliance/dpa/AP Images, 52–53; Claudio Divizia/Shutterstock, 54; Pictures from History/Universal Images Group/Getty Images, 59; Martin Zwick/Reda & Co./Universal Images Group/Getty Images, 60; Matthias Schrader/AP Images, 65; Mikhail Markovskiy/Shutterstock, 66–67; Hanns J. Jaeger/AP Images, 68; Patrik Stollarz/AFP/Getty Images, 71; Uli Deck/Picture Alliance/dpa/AP Images, 73; T. Lesia/Shutterstock, 76; Bernd von Jutrczenka/Picture Alliance/dpa/AP Images, 77; Albert Harlingue/Roger-Viollet/Getty Images, 78–79; Sanden Jr./AP Images, 80; AP Images, 82; Leonid Andronov/Shutterstock, 86; Onjira Leibe/Shutterstock, 90–91; Bernd W'stneck/Picture Alliance/dpa/AP Images, 94; Roland Weihrauch/Picture Alliance/dpa/AP Images, 95; Michael Sohn/AP Images, 96, 98

Editor: Marie Pearson
Series Designer: Maggie Villaume

Library of Congress Control Number: 2022940308

PUBLISHER'S CATALOGING-IN-PUBLICATION DATA
Names: Foran, Racquel, author.
Title: Germany / by Racquel Foran
Description: Minneapolis, Minnesota: Abdo Publishing, 2023 | Series: Essential Library of Countries | Includes online resources and index.
Identifiers: ISBN 9781532199417 (lib. bdg.) | ISBN 9781098274610 (ebook)
Subjects: LCSH: Germany--Juvenile literature. | Europe--Juvenile literature. | Germany--History--Juvenile literature. | Geography--Juvenile literature.
Classification: DDC 943.0--dc23

CONTENTS

CHAPTER **ONE**

A TOUR OF GERMANY

Looking out the airplane window, Kurt could hardly contain his excitement. He had been waiting his whole life to visit Germany, and the day had finally arrived. He and his family were flying into Berlin, the capital of Germany. Berlin is in eastern Germany, close to Poland's border. It had been a long eight-hour flight from New York, and he was ready to explore.

As the plane approached Berlin Brandenburg Airport Willy Brandt, Kurt could see a patchwork of green, lush land broken up by lakes, rivers, and canals. The landscape then transitioned to low-rise buildings with colorful rooftops. He began to see the larger

The Spree River flows through Berlin. People can enjoy river cruises and see landmarks such as the Berlin Cathedral, *left*, and the Fernsehturm TV tower, *right*.

In 2020, there were 1,528 active breweries in Germany.[1]

concrete block buildings of Berlin's city center interspersed with parks and gardens that softened their stark appearance.

Kurt's *Oma* and *Opa*—grandmother and grandfather—picked his family up at the airport. Brandenburg Airport was only a 30-minute drive to their home. Kurt and his family had a busy vacation ahead of them, and he could hardly wait to get started. As they drove from the airport, Kurt watched the passing landscape. The highway crossed the Spree River, and he could see bright kayaks dotting the water and picnickers lining the riverbank. Kurt imagined delicious homemade bread in their baskets.

They stopped at his uncle's *Bräuhaus*, a German brew house, before going to his Oma and Opa's. Kurt's family had been making beer in Germany for more than 150 years. His uncle used old family recipes to open a Bräuhaus in Opa's name. The restaurant also served bratwursts and sauerkraut from Kurt's great-grandmother's recipes. Bratwurst is a traditional German sausage. Sauerkraut is made with chopped and fermented cabbage. It has a sour taste and is a popular German side dish. Kurt's mouth watered just thinking about a delicious German meal.

BERLIN'S TIERGARTEN

After eating a meal at the Bräuhaus, Kurt and his family headed across the street to Tiergarten Park. Tiergarten is Berlin's largest and most frequently visited inner-city park. Kurt was ready to explore all it offered. Tiergarten has a long history. The 630-acre (255 ha) space was once a hunting ground for royalty.[2] In the late 1600s, Frederick III, Duke of Prussia, turned the grounds into a park for everyone. Like the rest of Germany, bombing during World War II (1939–1945) heavily damaged the park. Restoration began in 1949.

When they arrived, the lushness and diverse offerings of Tiergarten awed Kurt. The former hunting ground has become a hub for leisure and cultural activities and a place for remembrance and reconciliation in the city's heart for everyone to enjoy. There was a lot to see, including the Soviet War Memorial and the Haus der Kulturen der Welt (meaning "House of World Cultures") arts and exhibition center. The Memorial to the Murdered Jews of Europe is also in the park. It stands in remembrance of the millions of Jewish people killed by Germany's Nazi Party during World War II. Kurt stopped in

Tourists and locals alike enjoy nature in Tiergarten. Visitors bike, inline skate, jog, walk, and relax in the park.

his tracks as they approached the memorial. He had seen nothing like it. Massive cold concrete slabs stretched in all directions as far as his eye could see. There were no words or signs, just acres of concrete on the edge of a park. It was stark and startling and made Kurt shiver thinking about the lost lives the memorial honored.

THE REICHSTAG

Kurt and his family left Oma and Opa's house on day two to visit the Reichstag, home to Germany's parliament. When they arrived at its entrance, Kurt looked up to read the inscription above the door, "*Dem Deutschen Volke*," which translates to "To the German People." The Reichstag housed the German parliament until 1933, when fire damaged it. The building was further damaged during World War II. The government completed a full restoration of the building in 1999, and it began business in the building later that year.

The Reichstag now stands as a symbol of transparency, democracy, and sustainability. The family rode the elevator to the top of the enormous glass dome that sits above the parliamentary debate chambers. A debate was in session. Even though he could not hear what they were

MEMORIAL TO THE MURDERED JEWS OF EUROPE

The Memorial to the Murdered Jews of Europe, also known as the Holocaust Memorial, is a somber sight in the heart of Berlin. Covering 4.7 acres (1.9 ha), the memorial is composed of 2,711 concrete slabs of different heights.[3] Designed by New York architect Peter Eisenman, the memorial is a place to contemplate and remember. The memorial also serves to warn against future atrocities.

Architect Carl G. Langhans designed the Brandenburg Gate. He modeled it after the architecture from Athens, Greece.

saying, Kurt found it exciting to see government in action. While Kurt was engrossed in what was happening below, his mother was lost in the view outside. The glass dome offered a 360-degree view of Berlin. Kurt could hear his mom pointing out various sites to his sister, including Museum Island and a garden in full bloom. She loved the view so much they decided they would return to watch the sunset from high above the city.

UNTER DEN LINDEN

From the Reichstag, the family walked to the Brandenburg Gate. King Frederick William II commissioned the stone gate. It stands 66 feet (20 m) tall, 213 feet (65 m) wide, and 36 feet (11 m) deep.[4] Twelve columns create five portals. Two small buildings stand on either side of the gate. A statue of the goddess of victory bearing a symbol of peace tops the gate. Completed in 1791, it was to be made to be a grand end to the Unter den Linden promenade. The name of this 0.9-mile (1.5 km) pathway translates to "under the linden trees" after the linden trees that once grew there.[5] Kurt passed shops, cafés, and other buildings, such as Humboldt University and Staatsoper Unter den Linden—the Berlin opera house.

At the end of the promenade, they arrived at Museum Island, a United Nations Educational, Scientific and Cultural Organization (UNESCO) World Heritage site. It is home to several museums. They visited the Old Museum. As soon as they passed through the massive 18 pillars that create the entrance to the building, they split up. Kurt's sister wanted to see the museum's treasure vault of valuable jewels and gemstones. His mom and dad were going to check out the busts of Caesar and Cleopatra first. But Kurt's priority was to see the coins. He was obsessed with ancient coins

STAATSOPER

Completed in 1743, the Staatsoper Unter den Linden nearly burned to the ground in 1843 and suffered severe damage twice during World War II but was rebuilt each time. The German government began extensive restorations of the building in 2010, which included raising the roof to improve acoustics. Perhaps the most renowned of the opera house's stage settings for performances is the gold stars and dark blue night backdrop from Wolfgang Amadeus Mozart's opera *The Magic Flute*.

THE BERLIN WALL

Between 1949 and 1961, 2.5 million people left East Germany for West Germany. Many of these people were skilled workers and professionals. Berlin was their gateway to the West. To put an end to this, the GDR built a wall around West Berlin. The concrete wall was 15 feet (4.5 m) tall and topped with barbed wire. It ran 28 miles (45 km) between East and West Berlin and another 75 miles (120 km) around West Berlin's borders.[6] The wall was heavily guarded. During the 29 years it stood, more than 600 people died trying to cross the wall to West Berlin, including some whom GDR border guards killed.[7]

and minting, and the Old Museum has the best collection in the world.

When they left the museum, Kurt could feel his dad's mood change. They were heading to the Berlin Wall Memorial. The countries that defeated Germany in World War II divided the nation. From 1949 to 1989, it was two nation states: the Federal Republic of Germany (FRG), also called West Germany, and the German Democratic Republic (GDR), also called East Germany. The eastern side was under communist rule for 40 years. Berlin, located in East Germany, was similarly split in two, with communist control of the eastern portion. In 1961, the GDR built a wall around West Berlin, essentially blocking its citizens from escaping East German territory.

Kurt's dad had told him all about the day the wall came down. Growing up in East Germany, his dad did not enjoy basic freedoms like reading what he wanted, watching the movies he liked, or being allowed to travel. It was difficult for Kurt to imagine what that was like. After negotiations that began in late 1989, the two sides of the country reunited through a treaty signed on September 12, 1990. Citizens on both sides rushed to the wall to both destroy and climb it.

Part of the Berlin Wall has been turned into an art gallery.

The day the wall fell, it opened a whole new world of opportunity for Kurt's uncle, dad, and many other young East Germans. Their family trip was the first time his dad had visited since he left Germany a year after the wall fell. Kurt was glad he got to share the visit with his dad.

In 2022, there were more than 7,000 museums and exhibition houses in Germany.[8]

BEYOND BERLIN

Berlin is only one of several major cities in Germany, each offering something different to appreciate. On day three of the family's trip, they hit the road for the port city of Hamburg. When they climbed out of the car, Kurt could see their tour boat already waiting at the busy dock. He didn't know where to look first. Hamburg is the busiest port in Germany. Cargo ships lined the port, and the docks were stacked hundreds of feet high with brightly colored cargo containers. Massive cranes loomed overhead, plucking containers from one pile and swinging them onto waiting ships. Truck engines roared and boat horns blew.

The bustling port was fun, but Kurt was also excited for the rest of their trip. There was so much to see beyond the big cities. Germany is filled with quaint towns, relaxing resorts, and hundreds of spas. He was especially looking forward to the lakes, valleys, and castles of the Black Forest region. He thought it was cool that they would travel the same roads and pass through some of the same villages as people did in ancient times.

Hochburg Castle is in the Black Forest region. It was built in the 1000s CE.

YOUNG COUNTRY, LONG HISTORY

The history and culture of the German people go back thousands of years. The country now known as Germany was first unified in 1871 with land borders similar to what they are today. However, the united, economically thriving modern Germany is a young country. The thirtieth anniversary of the reunification of the FRG and GDR was October 3, 2020.

Germany's long and complex history is seen and felt everywhere. The government has restored old buildings to their former glory but also updated them with new and innovative design elements while leaving historical scars as a reminder of the past. Roads and alleys now lined by some of the most luxurious cars in the world follow the same paths carts and horses once traveled hundreds of years ago.

The land is as diverse and complex as the architecture and people. From the shores of the North and Baltic Seas in north Germany to the high mountain ranges of the Bavarian Alps in the south and the dense forest and picturesque villages of the Black Forest region in the southwest, the geography of Germany offers climates, settings, and adventures to satisfy visitors and residents alike.

CHAPTER **TWO**

GEOGRAPHY

Germany covers 137,847 square miles (357,022 sq km).[1] The country is landlocked on three sides and borders nine countries, the most of any western European nation. Austria and Switzerland are its two southern neighbors. The Netherlands, Belgium, and Luxembourg make up its western border. Its border with France stretches along the southwest side of the country. Germany shares its southeast border with the Czech Republic and its easternmost border with Poland. In the north on the Jutland peninsula, Germany borders Denmark. The Baltic Sea sits east of the peninsula and the North Sea sits to the west, completing the northern border.

Germany has many different landscapes, from coastlines to forests and mountain peaks.

There are three national parks on Germany's coast of the Wadden Sea: one each in the states of Schleswig-Holstein, Hamburg, and Lower Saxony.

COASTLINES AND RIVERS

Germany's northern coastline extends along the North Sea and Baltic Sea. The coast is mostly shallow, made up of marshes, dunes, or beach walls. Only a small portion is steep terrain. Germans know the coast for its *steife Brise*, or "stiff breeze."

The North Sea is larger than the Baltic Sea, and its German shoreline shifts with the changing tides. Depending on the time of year, the landscape can look completely different. The Wadden Sea runs along the coast from Denmark to the Netherlands, including the German Wadden Sea National Parks. The Wadden Sea is the longest system of intertidal sand and mud flats in the world. A UNESCO Natural World Heritage site, it covers 2.8 million acres (1.1 million ha). This mostly undisturbed stretch is one of the world's most important areas for

Jasmund National Park has the largest chalk cliffs in Germany, with the highest parts reaching 528 feet (161 m) above the Baltic Sea.

migratory birds. Visitors can see six million birds at the same time in the Wadden Sea. Between ten and 12 million birds pass through the region each year.[2]

The Frisian Islands form an archipelago off the coast in the North Sea. The mudflats between them and the mainland are often exposed at low tide. Channels cut through these flats, including the estuaries that feed the Elbe and Weser Rivers. The region can be very cold in the fall and winter, but in spring and summer kite surfing, horse riding, and swimming are popular activities for vacationers.

The Baltic Sea is deep and marked by fjords with steep banks. It is a popular area for sailing and fishing, and many fishing villages line the coast. The area is famous for its chalk cliffs above the beach, framed by a backdrop of ancient beech-tree forests. The ancient beech forests of Jasmund National Park on the island Rügen in the Baltic Sea were added to the UNESCO World Heritage List in 2011.

Eleven major rivers crisscross the German landscape. Germans rely on this network of rivers for commerce, tourism, and leisure. The Rhine, Ems,

UPPER MIDDLE RHINE VALLEY

The Rhine River has served as a connection between northern and southern Europe for centuries. UNESCO has added a 40-mile (65 km) stretch of the Rhine River Valley to the World Heritage List for its role in history and legend and for its influence on writers, artists, and composers. The prosperity of this transportation route is reflected in landscape. Sixty small towns line this short stretch, and vineyard terraces cover the hillsides. Approximately 40 castles and forts stare down on the land and river below.[3] Because of preservation and conservation efforts, the landscape of this stretch of the valley remains mostly untouched.

THE WINE REGIONS OF GERMANY

Germany has 13 wine regions, most in the southwest corner of the country in the states of Baden-Württemberg and Rhineland-Palatinate.[5] The Ahr is the northernmost wine-growing region. Here several miles of vineyards line the Ahr River. Baden is in the southernmost region. Tucked between the Black Forest and Rhine River, this region gets some of the sunniest weather in the country. Rheinhessen is Germany's largest wine-growing region. It is also home to Germany's oldest known vineyard, Niersteiner Glöck. Part of the parish of Saint Mary's Church since before 742 CE, the Glöck still grows Riesling and Gewürztraminer grapes.

Weser, Saale, and Elbe Rivers all flow north and drain into the North Sea. The Neckar, the Main, and the Moselle are tributaries of the Rhine, feeding it in the summer. Commercially, the Rhine is one of the most important rivers in Europe. Its source is Lake Toma in Switzerland. It flows through several German cities and the countries of Austria and France before it drains into the North Sea from the Netherlands.

The Danube slices across the southern half of the country, starting in the Black Forest and flowing southeast before draining into the Black Sea in Romania. The Danube is the second-longest river in Europe at 1,777 miles (2,859 km) long. It is also a source of water for more than 20 million people. More than six million tourists visit it each year.[4]

PLAINS, VALLEYS, AND MOUNTAINS

Germany's topography rises upward from north to south. The North German Plain is part of a large European plain that spans from France to Russia. In Germany, the lowlands begin at the ocean's edge as a puzzle of mudflats, lagoons, marshes, and moors. The land slowly transitions to rolling hills. At their highest, the hills reach only 656 feet (200 m) above sea level, but most are less than 330 feet (100 m).[6] The hills of the southern edge of the plain have excellent drainage. One-third of Germany's land is arable, meaning it is good for growing crops. Some of it is in these hills. This fertile soil combined with a moderate climate and long growing season makes this region Germany's breadbasket, which is the fertile agricultural region of a country where most of its crops are grown.

The Central German Uplands are heavily forested. On the north side, the topography is layers of rock. Mountains rise from this rock. With peaks reaching approximately 2,952 feet (900 m), this region offers some breathtaking river valley views where the Rhine and Moselle Rivers cut through the mountains.[7]

The region of Bavaria sits in the Alpine Foreland that leads to the foothills of the Alps. Most of the area is rural, but the city of Munich is in this region. The mountains of the Alps run across the southern length of the country along the Swiss and Austrian borders. The Allgäuer Alps are the westernmost range in Germany, the Bavarian Alps form the central range, and the Salzburg Limestone Alps make up the eastern end.

Tucked between the central uplands and the Alpine Foreland lies southern Germany. The Black Forest is in this region. It covers 2,320 square miles (6,009 sq km) and runs along the Rhine River for 100 miles (160 km).[8] In addition to its lush landscape and many quaint towns, the Black Forest region is famous for its mineral springs and spas.

MAP OF GERMANY

KEY:

- Capital
- City
- Point of Interest

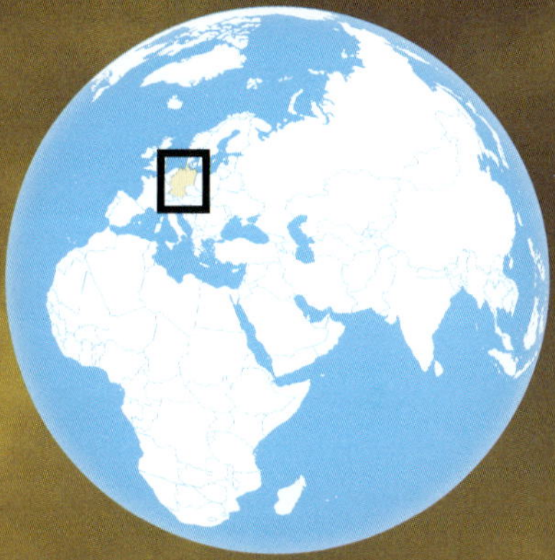

Hohenzollern Castle is near the city of Hechingen in southwest Germany. In January, the average low temperature in the city is about 28 degrees Fahrenheit (–2°C).

CLIMATE AND SEASONS

Germany's seasons are characterized by its continental climate. The country experiences clearly defined seasons following the same calendar as the United States. The winter months are cold, and the summer months are hot.

The winter months of December through March can see temperatures dip below freezing, but they usually hover around 32 degrees Fahrenheit (0°C) or a little warmer. Cities such as Hamburg and Bremen in the northern region can be slightly warmer in the winter, but because of their proximity to the ocean, they get more rain and heavy winds. In the mountainous terrain of the Alps, the temperature can drop several degrees below freezing.

Spring weather arrives late. The season begins on March 21, but the weather does not get significantly warmer for another few weeks. By May, flowers are in bloom and the weather is quite pleasant. Average temperatures in the summer are approximately

At 9,721 feet (2,963 m) above sea level, the Zugspitze Mountain in the Bavarian Alps is the highest peak in Germany.[9]

75 degrees Fahrenheit (24°C), with the south being warmer than the north. With so much of the country covered in forests and nature parks, the land comes alive with the vibrant colors of fall. Temperatures are mild in early fall.

The direction the wind blows has a significant impact on the weather in all seasons. Winds from the North Sea and North Atlantic bring cool temperatures. Winds coming from the southwest are warmer and bring mild weather. Sometimes an Arctic front will swoop in from the north, bringing with it freezing temperatures. The winds change often and quickly, which makes the weather unpredictable. Fog, thunderstorms, snow, rain, tornadoes, and occasionally hurricanes all blow in with the winds.

Rainfall in Germany depends on the region. The low plains around Berlin in the east see the least amount of precipitation a year with between 20 and 30 inches (50 to 76 cm). The Alpine region gets the most precipitation, with more than 80 inches (200 cm) of precipitation each year.[10] The average hours of sunshine each year also depend on the region, from 1,467 hours a year in Lower Saxony to 1,805 hours in Baden-Württemberg.[11]

FAIRY TALE ROUTE

The Fairy Tale Route begins in Hanau on the Main River. It is the birthplace of the Brothers Grimm, who compiled "Hansel and Gretel," "Snow White and the Seven Dwarfs," and many other well-known fairy tales. The route follows the life of the brothers 370 miles (595 km) north up the Weser River to the port city of Bremen.[12] Along the way travelers pass through towns such as Hameln, where the tale of the Pied Piper took place, and a section along the Schwalm River that Germans have named Rotkäppchenland, or "Little Red Riding Hood Country."

Hamburg's location on the Elbe River makes it important for shipping.

URBAN SPACES

There are five major cities in Germany. Berlin in the east is the capital and largest city by population, with more than 3.6 million people. The port city of Hamburg in the north has a population of more than 1.8 million. Munich in the Bavarian region is home to almost 1.5 million people. Cologne in the west has a population of more than one million. The city of Frankfurt am Main, home to the country's financial district, has more than 750,000 residents.[13]

In 2016, Germany had 2,059 cities and towns. Nearly 100 cities had a population of 100,000 or more. More than 1,500 cities had a population of more than 10,000.[14] In 2020, Germany was the fifth-most densely populated country in the European Union.[15]

CHAPTER **THREE**

PLANTS AND ANIMALS

Germany's diverse landscapes create habitats for a variety of plants and animals. There are thousands of species living in the country. Agricultural development has been the greatest threat to plants and animals. Approximately 26 percent of native plants and 35 percent of native animals are endangered.[1]

ANIMALS

There are 48,000 animal species in Germany. Of those, 33,000 are insects.[2] Common insects found throughout the country include the violet carpenter bee, the seven-spotted ladybird, and the Apollo

The chamois, a small goat antelope, is one of many animal species living in Germany.

and admiral butterflies. Forests are home to game animals such as deer, wild boars, quails, and pheasants. The European wildcat and European badger are also native to Germany. The mountains above the tree line are habitat for a goat antelope called the chamois and the alpine ibex, a wild mountain goat of the Alps. Red foxes are abundant, and they roam forests and towns alike, hunting rabbits and rodents.

Brown bears and gray wolves were both considered extinct in Germany starting in the 1800s. In the 1990s, gray wolves were reintroduced to the German wild. By 2022, there were between 1,300 and 1,800 wolves living in the northeastern region of Germany.[3] Bears remained extinct, but a few sightings in the early 2020s left some hopeful they also might return to the German wild.

The seas and islands of the north coast are home to harbor seals, gray seals, and harbor porpoises. Beavers and otters live in the rivers of Germany. One prized but threatened species of the river is the huchen fish. Also known as the Danube salmon, it grows up to six feet (1.8 m) long.[4]

WILD MUSHROOMS

The German Mycological Society estimates there are 14,000 species of mushrooms growing in Germany.[5] And German people are wild for *Waldpilze*, meaning "forest mushrooms." Many species are poisonous, but the ones that are not are popular menu items throughout the fall. The tastiest varieties became so popular they were over picked. This led to mushroom-picking restrictions and heavy fines for those caught breaking the rules. People cannot pick wild mushrooms for profit, and each day they can pick only what they can personally consume in a day. Only people with a special license for scientific research can pick certain varieties, such as truffles.

Northern gannets can dive at a speed of up to 54 miles per hour (86 kmh). They can also dive as deep as 72 feet (22 m) underwater.

Once abundant throughout the Danube River watershed, it now spawns in only a few areas.

Among the species of birds that live in Germany, there are northern gannets, kittiwakes, and guillemots, which build their nests and lay their

In May 2022, there were 552 confirmed species of birds in Germany.[6]

eggs on the high cliffs of Helgoland, an island in the North Sea. The golden eagle flies high above the Alps. Although not endangered, it is at risk of becoming endangered.

WILD BOAR PROBLEM

In 2021, African swine fever (ASF) crossed the Polish border and spread to wild boar in Germany. Although not a danger to humans, it kills every infected pig within ten days. This was a major concern for the country because the disease spreads easily, putting Germany's pig farmers at risk. Germany is Europe's biggest pork producer. It erected hundreds of miles of fencing to keep the disease from spreading further in the country, but cases were later found beyond the fencing. In March 2022, regulators confirmed hundreds of cases of ASF in wild boars in eastern Germany along the Polish border.

FORESTS, TREES, AND PLANTS

Germany has approximately 10,300 species of plants.[7] German forests have survived many dangers over the centuries. Heavy use of forests for timber and fuel through the mid-1700s led to massive deforestation. The fertile plains of Germany were once covered in oak and hornbeam forests. The sandy areas of this region were a mix of oak and birch woodland. But agricultural development stripped these regions of their forests and replaced them with fields of heather for grazing sheep. By the early 1800s, extensive areas of German forest were bare. The country had reached an all-time low in forest cover. To prevent a timber shortage, foresters developed the framework for sustainable forest management. It created land reforms and reshaped the use of forests, which led to reforestation. The forest began to recover, but two world wars in 30 years did major damage to them again.

From 2015 to 2020, Germany's forests lost a yearly average of nearly 17,300 acres (7,000 ha) to deforestation.

Forests play an important role in the economy, lifestyle, and culture of the country. The German government has committed to restoring them. It has taken dedication and time to recover their health and size. Forests now cover one-third of Germany.[8] The replanted forests include different trees from what grew originally. Some of the northern German plain now has Scotch pine. Beech trees once dominated the forests of the uplands, but over the years, non-native trees have been added to the mix. Species of Weymouth pines, Douglas firs, and Japanese larches were introduced. Spruces, pines, beeches, and oaks are among the common trees. Fir trees dominate the Black Forest.

Other parts of the country offer different plant life. Sea lavender is hardy enough to survive salty air and grows along the North Sea coast. Sea thistle grows in the dunes. And high in the Alps, the mountains come alive with color when the gentian and edelweiss bloom. In the orchards of the fertile plains, apple, pear, cherry, and plum trees are among the fruit trees grown.

THE BLACK FOREST

The Black Forest is in the state of Baden-Württemberg in southwest Germany. It is one of the most picturesque areas of Germany. Extending northeast from the Upper Rhine River at the Swiss border, it covers 2,320 square miles (6,008 sq km).[9] The forest gets its name from the dark evergreens that loom over its expanse, but there is nothing gloomy about the Black Forest. Storybook towns, patchwork farmland, and lush vineyards fill its river valleys. In the northwest corner of the forest, there are natural hot springs that have been a spa destination for 2,000 years.

PARKS AND GREEN SPACES

Germany prizes its parks and green spaces as much as its forests. In 2022, there were 16 national parks.[10] There were also 16 biosphere reserves, which are protected natural areas for researching conservation while also meeting land use needs. And there were 100 nature parks. Together, all these parks and green spaces covered one-quarter of the country's land.[11] In 2007, the federal government adopted the National Strategy on Biological Diversity. It committed to designating 2 percent of land to large-scale wilderness areas and 5 percent to be preserved as permanently unused forests.[12]

In 2017, several government ministries produced a paper entitled "Green Spaces in the City," which made ten recommendations of action for the government to take to ensure urban areas have green spaces.

The willow gentian is one of the gentian species that grow in Germany.

Allotment gardens are an important part of urban green spaces. They are small gardens for people to grow their own fruits and vegetables. These gardens have a 150-year history in Germany. In 1983, the government introduced an act to protect and promote these gardens for generations to come. In 2022, more than 4.5 million Germans cared for approximately one million allotment gardens.[13]

The capital city of Berlin is one of the most nature-filled cities in Europe. More than 30 percent of the city is green spaces and woodland.[14] Besides extensive parks, urban forests, and allotment gardens, spaces once occupied by the Berlin Wall grow wild 30 years after its fall. In addition, when the Tempelhof Airport closed in 2008, its grassy areas and pavement remained for all Berliners to use.

People can grow a variety of plants, including flowers and produce, in allotment gardens.

CHAPTER **FOUR**

HISTORY

Germany is a young country. It officially unified in 1871. The history of the Germanic people, however, long predates the formation of the nation's modern-day borders. People who spoke Germanic languages may have lived within the area that is now Germany for thousands of years. There is archaeological evidence that these people occupied the northern region of modern Germany while Celtic people occupied the southern region. Germanic people began moving southward between 100 BCE and 100 CE. During this period, the people of the southern region gradually became Germanized.

When Julius Caesar's Roman army arrived in the region in 50 BCE, the soldiers found a melting pot of

Artifacts such as sculptures and weapons have helped archaeologists learn more about Germanic peoples' religions and ways of life.

A carving on a Roman coffin shows Roman and Germanic warriors fighting.

Germanic and Celtic people. Caesar formed the province of Gaul on the west side of the Rhine River. Germanic people lived on both sides of the river. Caesar called the region east of the river Germania. The Germanic people lived in many independent tribes, including Saxons, Franks, and Bavarians, and they cultivated the land. Over time, tribes banded together to form larger tribes. Together, these tribes did not form a nation but an informal grouping of many independent states that lasted for hundreds of years.

There were battles between the Germanic tribes and the Romans. Roman general Nero Claudius Drusus Germanicus fought to conquer Germanic territory across the Rhine from 12 to 9 BCE. The tribes put up fierce battles. In 9 BCE, Germanic tribal leader Arminius surprised the Romans, and his army defeated the Romans at the battle of Teutoburg Forest. The Romans recognized a strong opponent, so for a period they settled their borders east along the Rhine and Danube Rivers and south of the Elbe River.

Archaeological evidence shows that the territory of the Germanic people covered a vast area for a time. It spanned from the Rhine River in western Germany to the Vistula River in Poland, and from Scandinavia in the north to the Carpathian Mountains in the southeast. From 50 CE to approximately 350 CE, the Germanic people coexisted with the Romans. They lived in wood structures and established an agricultural system. Unlike the Romans, these tribes did not have a monetary system.

Historians have found evidence at burial sites that social class structures were forming among

LIFESTYLE OF EARLY GERMANIC TRIBES

Early Germanic tribes lived on farmsteads where people and animals lived together in longhouses. Buildings were made from wood and clay. People grew grains and vegetables and kept animals for both food and hides. These people had granaries for storing grain. They also had workshops. Everything the people needed was produced and made on the farmstead, including food, clothes, and tools. Instead of using a monetary system, they traded with the Romans, giving them things like animal skins, amber, and honey in exchange for weapons, jewelry, and glass.

The Palatine Chapel in Aachen, built between 793 and 813, is a surviving part of Charlemagne's Palace of Aachen.

the various Germanic tribes during this time. Tribes banded together to form leagues. The leagues came together to worship, share cultural activities, engage in trade and commerce, and resolve disputes. Some tribes settled along the shores of the Rhine River and had regular interaction with the Romans. Wealthy Germanic graves included Roman luxuries like fine glass and pottery. Some Germanic people became Roman slaves and warriors. By 117 CE, the Romans again controlled northern Europe. German cities such as Bonn and Cologne get their names from Latin, the language of the Romans.

From about 150 to 200, Germanic tribes were on the move again. They traveled from Scandinavia south along river valleys into Roman territory, waging a destructive war with the Roman Empire. In 251, the Goths, Germanic people from southern Scandinavia, killed Roman emperor Decius. War raged in the Danube and Rhine regions until 280, when the Romans formed alliances with the Frank, Alemanni, and Goth tribes. Stability lasted until about 370.

CHANGING RULERS

The Franks started building an empire in western Europe in the 400s. One of the most famous Frank rulers was Charlemagne. His goal was to unite all Germanic people and convert them to Christianity. During his rule from 768 to 814, he conquered even more territory for the Franks. In 800, the pope named Charlemagne the Holy Roman emperor. Francis II (1768–1835) was an emperor of Austria and was also the last Holy Roman emperor. Between 1792 and 1806, Francis

II went to war with France three times. After Francis II's final defeat in 1806, the French leader Napoléon Bonaparte dissolved the Holy Roman Empire, and Francis II abdicated his throne.

In 1813, the German state of Prussia, along the southwest Baltic Sea, drove France out of its region. At the Congress of Vienna that was held between 1814 and 1815 to reorganize Europe, participants decided to divide Germany into 39 states.[1] It was a loose union with no central seat of power. Regional leaders met at a federal assembly that Austria ruled. But this did not last long. In 1866, the Seven Weeks' War between Austria and Prussia broke out, with Prussia emerging victorious. The prime minister of Prussia, Otto von Bismarck, formed the North German Confederation. But he had a goal of unifying all Germany. Next, to gain the support of the people in southern Germany, he provoked a war with France. The Germans won the war, and the south agreed to join a united Germany. In 1871, he achieved his goal and the German nation, with its current-day borders, was born. Germany quickly became a superpower, engaging in overseas trade and colonization. But its neighbors did not like or trust their new powerful neighbor. Countries formed alliances in case war broke out.

WORLD WAR I

On June 28, 1914, a Bosnian Serb and Slavic nationalist named Gavrilo Princip assassinated Archduke Franz Ferdinand, heir to the throne of Austria-Hungary. It was all the provocation that was needed to start what would become World War I (1914–1918). The Austro-Hungarians wanted to retaliate against Serbia. Germany and Turkey sided with Austria-Hungary to form the Central

***Arrest of a Suspect in Sarajevo* is a famous photograph from the day Archduke Franz Ferdinand was assassinated. At the time, the person arrested was thought to be Gavrilo Princip, the assassin. But after decades of scholarly debate, the photographed man is thought to be an innocent bystander.**

powers. Russia, France, Britain, and later Japan and the United States, supported Serbia. On July 28, Austria-Hungary declared war on Serbia. The following day, it bombed the city of Belgrade, Serbia. On July 30, Russia mobilized its forces. On August 1, Germany declared war against Russia, and on August 3, it declared war against France. By August 28, Austria-Hungary had also declared war on Russia, Japan, and Belgium. Serbia, Montenegro, and Japan had all declared war against Germany.

On April 26, 1915, Russia, Britain, and France signed the Treaty of London, uniting them as the Allies. The Allies had advantages over the Central powers. They had greater military and industrial resources and better access to oceans and neutral trade partners. Still, the war raged far longer than expected. In April 1917, after having suffered the loss of many merchant ships and civilians, the United States declared war on Germany. The infusion of American troops contributed to the end of the war 20 months later. On November 11, 1918, Germany signed an armistice agreement with the Allies, and the war ended.

WORLD WAR II

After World War I ended, the Allied powers forced Germany to sign the Treaty of Versailles. The treaty required Germany to pay financial damages and give up vast territory, among other things. This, combined with the destruction of the war, left Germany economically devastated. The country sank into a deep financial depression. Businesses closed, people lost their jobs, and banks failed. The German people were angry with their government. They were desperate and looking for a powerful leader to lift them out of despair. A man named Adolf Hitler entered the political scene with his Nazi Party and promised to restore Germany to what it considered the country's former glory. Hitler slowly built up his army and air force. In 1938, German troops entered German-speaking regions of Austria and Czechoslovakia. Shortly after, Hitler formed alliances with

Adolf Hitler gained supreme power as a dictator through intimidation and steady elimination of opposition.

Italy and Japan. The trio of nations was called the Axis powers.

The United Kingdom and France were not expecting or prepared for war, and for a time they tried to appease Hitler. They allowed him to annex a German-speaking region of Czechoslovakia. In exchange, he agreed not to encroach any farther into the country and not to invade any other countries. Hitler did not honor the agreement, though, and he invaded the rest of Czechoslovakia. On September 1, 1939, he invaded Poland. When he did this, the United Kingdom and France declared war against Germany. World War II had begun.

The war raged for six years, drawing in more countries. The United States, the Soviet Union, and China joined the United Kingdom and France to become the Allies. Fifty nations were in battle, with more than 100 million soldiers.[2] In April 1945, Allied troops closed in on Berlin. Sensing his defeat, Hitler died by suicide on April 30, bringing an end to his rule. World War II finally ended in Europe on May 8, 1945, when Germany surrendered. Between 35 and 60 million people died in World War II.[3] This included approximately six million Jews whom Hitler had murdered in Nazi concentration camps.[4]

THE HOLOCAUST

German Nazi leader Adolf Hitler had racist, discriminatory, and anti-Semitic beliefs. He considered Jews, Romani people, homosexuals, people with intellectual disabilities, and dissidents of any kind all to be inferior people and a threat to the purity of the German race. Between 1933 and 1945, Hitler and his Nazi Party sanctioned and sponsored the persecution and mass murder of approximately six million Jewish men, women, and children, as well as five million other people he targeted for political, religious, or racial reasons.[5] This horrific event is called the Holocaust.

Volunteers in Germany worked to clear rubble after World War II.

TWO GERMANYS

The end of World War II did not bring peace or unity. Allied powers continued an uneasy alliance, with each country having its own ideas and motives about what postwar Europe should look like. The one thing they agreed on was decentralizing the power of Germany's government and the demilitarization and denazification of Germany. Again, Germany was required to pay financial

> **Germany had an estimated 6.6 to 8.8 million deaths from World War II.**[6]

damages and give up territory. As a temporary measure, the Allies divided the country. The Americans, British, and French occupied the western two-thirds of the country. It became the Federal Republic of Germany (FRG), or West Germany. The Soviets occupied the eastern third, which surrounded Berlin. It was called the German Democratic Republic (GDR), or more commonly East Germany. What was meant to be temporary instead lasted 40 years. West Germany joined Western democracy. East Germany, along with the Soviet Union and its bordering nations to the west, formed a communist bloc that alienated and isolated its people from western nations. One of the most extreme measures of this era was the East German construction of the Berlin Wall, physically blocking passage between East and West.

The war left Germany devastated in other ways too. The war destroyed a significant amount of the housing in many cities. Factories, hospitals, and transportation systems were gone. There were food shortages. Many Germans were homeless, and many more were suffering from malnutrition. This time in German history is called Zero Hour, when the country had to rebuild from nothing.

POSTWAR AND REUNIFICATION

The road to recovery was not equal for the two nations. West Germany embraced a free-market capitalist society that included strong government oversight and a social safety net. It introduced a new currency called the deutsche mark, lowered taxes, and removed government price controls.

UNIFICATION TREATY

After intense negotiations to peacefully reunite East and West Germany, the two sides signed a Unification Treaty on August 31, 1990. This treaty acknowledged the desire of the people from both parts of the country to live freely and in unity. It created a framework for dividing East Germany into five states, which then became part of the new Federal Republic of Germany. The treaty also addressed financial and legal issues to facilitate the merging of East Berlin into the new Federal Republic's systems.

These were controversial moves, but within six months, the country's industrial production had rapidly grown.

Things were not as good for East Germany. Its economy struggled to recover. The communist government imposed strict limits on citizens' freedom and movement. The people began protesting the government. Many tried to flee the country, and some died trying. In November 1989, the East German government allowed its citizens to travel to West Germany for the first time in 40 years. The number of people rushing to leave the country left the wall meaningless and led to its fall.

Once the government allowed East German citizens to access the west, the people demanded a greater say in politics. In March 1990, they held the first democratic election in East Germany since before World War II. The eastern Christian Democratic Union party ousted and replaced the ruling communist party. The new ruling party was a counterpart to the party of West German chancellor Helmut Kohl. The new East German government immediately began treaty negotiations to reunify the nation. On October 3, 1990, the two German nations ratified a unification treaty at the Bundestag in Berlin, and the new Federal Republic of Germany was born.

CHAPTER **FIVE**

PEOPLE AND CULTURE

For hundreds of years, Germany was the center of European culture. Some of the most celebrated composers, poets, and philosophers came from Germany, and their influence throughout Western culture remains. Germans often pride themselves as intellectuals and for being appreciative of the arts and literature.

An unofficial country slogan, *Ordnung muss sein*, means "there must be order." Germans often believe if people follow rules, things will be better for everyone. Germans sometimes have a reputation for being blunt, humorless perfectionists. At the same time, they have a strong sense of community and love a good beer

Some German cities hold light and music shows for the Day of German Unity.

Hamburg is one of Germany's most populated cities.

festival. They celebrate some of the same holidays that many people in North America do. New Year's Day, Easter, and Christmas Day are all federal holidays. On October 3, Germans celebrate their Day of German Unity, remembering the day in 1990 when the country was reunited.

DEMOGRAPHICS

Germany is the third-most-populated country in Europe after Russia and Turkey.[1] There are cities in all regions of the country, and in 2022, 77.6 percent of Germans lived in urban centers. More than 10 percent of Germany's people live in just five of the largest cities.[2]

The German birth rate is decreasing. Germany has the eleventh-lowest birth rate in the world, with nine births per 1,000 people in 2020. By comparison, the birth rate in the United States was 11 per 1,000 the same year.[3]

Germany's low birth rate means population growth has also stalled. Between 2019 and 2021, the population hovered at 83.2 million.[4] The number of deaths exceeded births in these years, but immigration offset this, leading to net zero population loss.

The median age of Germans in 2020 was 45.7. Retirees are living long after retirement, with a typical German expected to live to almost 82 years old.[5] With its aging population and declining birthrate, the nation will have to rely on immigration to replace its retiring workforce. In 2021, more than 86.3 percent of the population was German. The next largest ethnic group was Turkish at 1.8 percent, followed by Polish, Syrian, and Romanian at 1 percent each.[6]

LANGUAGE

German is the official language of Germany. Ninety-five percent of the German population speaks German.[7] There are regional dialects of German referred to as High and Low German. The written forms of High German and Low German differ little more than American and Canadian English, but they sound very different when spoken. High German, which originates from the southern highlands, is the official written language. It is what Germans use in academia, government, literature, and media. Germany is called Deutschland by locals, and they call their language Deutsch. The word *Deutsch* comes from the Old High German word *diutisc*, which means "of the people."

Low German is from the lowlands of northern Germany. Although still spoken in many homes in Northern Germany, it has no official status as a language. More than half the population of Germany also speaks English, and 27 percent of Germans speak two foreign languages.[8]

RELIGIONS

Germany has been at the center of religious upheaval and change for centuries. The Germanic people originally worshipped many local deities. Their conversion to Christianity took several centuries. The Goths started converting to Christianity as early as the 300s CE. Charlemagne's reign in the 700s brought Christianity to the Germanic people, and the German nation became one of the most powerful in the Holy Roman Empire. By 1054, tensions had risen between the branches of the church in the western and eastern regions, and the church split in two. Roman Catholicism prevailed in western Germany, and Eastern Orthodoxy emerged in the eastern region.

The next big religious change to happen in Germany was at the hands of Martin Luther, an Augustinian monk from Erfurt, Germany. Luther wanted to reform the Roman Catholic Church. Luther nailed his Ninety-Five Theses to a church door in Wittenberg, Germany, in 1517. This document outlined several practices of the Roman Catholic Church that Luther believed did not follow the Bible. The church attempted to get Luther to renounce his writings, but he refused. In January 1521, the church excommunicated Luther, meaning it formally expelled him. In response, Luther began a campaign to encourage not just religious change but also political and social change. In 1527, he established the Lutheran Church in Saxony. This was the beginning of the Christian religious movement Protestantism.

The Cologne Cathedral is one of many Roman Catholic churches in Germany.

In modern Germany, laws guarantee religious freedom and prohibit religious discrimination. Today, 40.7 percent of the population do not identify as religious. The split between Roman Catholics and Protestants is near equal, with 26.7 percent of the population identifying as Catholic and 24.3 percent identifying as Protestant. Muslims make up 3.5 percent of the population.[9] Church attendance is falling. Only 10 percent of registered Catholics and only 3 percent of registered Protestants attend services regularly.[10]

MUSIC AND DANCE

Music has long played an important role in German culture. German music falls into three broad categories: classic composers; folk music; and modern pop, rock, and *schlager*. Germany produced dozens of famous composers through history. An important early composer from Germany was the multitalented Saint Hildegard von Bingen (1098–1179). She has one of the largest collections of works of any Medieval composer, and dozens of pieces have survived. Germany's most celebrated composers are the "Three B's," Johann Sebastian Bach (1685–1750), Ludwig van Beethoven (1770–1827), and Johannes Brahms (1833–1897). Bach composed in the Baroque style and wrote for the organ and harpsichord. Beethoven was a star of the Classical era of music. He wrote everything from simple piano pieces to complex orchestra compositions. Brahms was a Romantic era pianist whose most famous work, "Lullaby," is a standard in nurseries. Several famed opera composers also came from Germany, such as Carl Maria von Weber and Richard Wagner. These people wrote some of the most famous operas of all time.

MINI **BIO**

LUDWIG VAN BEETHOVEN

One of the most famous German composers is Ludwig van Beethoven. Baptized December 17, 1770, in Bonn, Germany, Beethoven first gained attention as a youth when court organist Christian Gottlob Neefe became his teacher. He wrote his first composition in 1783.

Over the next several years, he gained many admirers among members of the aristocracy. In total, Beethoven wrote nine symphonies, 32 piano sonatas, 16 string quartets, an opera, and many other pieces. His more famous works include the opera *Fidelio*, the Piano Sonata no. 14 "Moonlight," and Symphony no. 9 in D Minor. In his late twenties, Beethoven began to experience ringing and buzzing in his ears. Within a decade, he was completely deaf, but he continued to compose until his death in 1827 in Vienna, Austria.

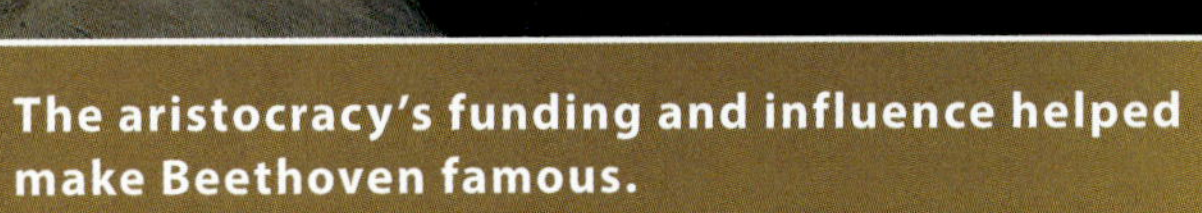

The aristocracy's funding and influence helped make Beethoven famous.

Volksmusik and oompah are the two types of traditional folk music most associated with Germany and its famous Oktoberfest. Volksmusik means "music of the people." It, along with the traditional Alpine hat and lederhosen the musicians wear, originates from the Bavarian region. The songs were originally about working-class issues or politics, and musicians played common instruments such as the guitar and harmonica. Oompah gets its name from the sound a tuba makes, a central instrument in all oompah bands. Along with the brass instruments, accordions add a unique sound to oompah bands. Yodeling is also German. The English word yodel comes from the German word *jodeln*, which means "to utter the syllable jo." Yodeling was used as a method of communication between villages divided by Alpine peaks. It is now performed for fun.

After World War II, schlager became the music of the people. Schlager is Germany's version of pop music that especially appealed to young people in the 1960s. It is light, fun, and not meant to be taken too seriously. *Volkstümliche Musik* is a modern style

LEDERHOSEN

Lederhosen are leather shorts with suspenders. They were traditionally worn by working-class people in the Bavarian region of Germany. During the 1700s, high society would copy things from peasants. Soon lederhosen became fashionable attire for the royal court. The working class wore simple lederhosen made from goat or sheep skin. The nobles made theirs from much softer deer skin. People of all classes embellished some lederhosen with embroidered designs. This embroidery symbolized specific regions, and people wore them with pride. In modern times, lederhosen are most often worn during Oktoberfest.

of schlager that mixes lyrics of traditional folk songs with modern drum machines and synthesizers. Music has always been important to young people in Germany. Today, genres such as German new wave, punk, techno-electronica, Medieval metal, hip-hop, and modern rock and pop are played in urban nightclubs and found on German playlists.

Germany has also had an influence on the world of dance. The waltz was born in southern Germany and Austria, and its popularity grew throughout Europe. The 1800s were the age of the Viennese waltz. Before the 1900s, Germans performed ballet mostly within opera performances. In the 1960s, the Stuttgart Ballet in Baden-Württemberg state gained world prominence, and it remains one of the premier ballet companies in the world. The Hamburg Ballet is also renowned. And Wuppertal is where dance theater was first introduced in the 1970s. Forty years after its founding, Tanztheater Wuppertal was still considered one of the top dance theater companies.

ART AND ARCHITECTURE

Because Germany was once composed of many small kingdoms, the country is dotted with castles. The European Castles Institute estimates there were 25,000 castles in Germany at one time. About 60 percent of those still stand, and ruins from many others are still open to explore.[11] One of Germany's oldest standing castles is Eltz Castle. Built in 1157 CE, it sits on the hills above the Moselle River and was continuously occupied for more than 800 years.

German architecture is renowned beyond its castles. Germany's churches and other historical buildings have also been influenced by diverse architectural styles including Gothic,

Renaissance, and Rococo styles. Postwar architecture is influenced by the Bauhaus school, which paired harmony of style with function by using beautiful materials and minimal decorative embellishments. In East Berlin, the influences of the communist regime that ruled for 40 years are apparent in the enormous, plain structures that still dominate the area. All these influences have combined with innovative new design styles, creating a unique architectural landscape.

SPAS

Spas play a significant role in German culture. The German people adopted the spa tradition from Roman soldiers, who used to stop in the natural hot springs of the Black Forest to bathe and soak their aching bodies after battle. They derived the word *spa* from Latin *sanus per aquam*, meaning "health by water."

In German, the prefix *bad* means "bath." A town can apply to add *bad* to its name, for example Bad Soden, if it meets exact air and water quality standards, and it must be able to provide medical

NEUSCHWANSTEIN CASTLE

One of Germany's most popular tourist attractions, Neuschwanstein Castle, attracts 1.3 million visitors each year.[12] King Louis II began construction in 1868. Building continued for more than 20 years, but it was never completed. Despite being modeled after medieval castles, Neuschwanstein is full of modern amenities. It has flushing toilets, hot and cold running water in the kitchen and bathrooms, a central forced-air heating system, an elevator between the kitchen and dining room, and even telephone lines. Sitting high on a rocky ledge in the Bavarian Alps, it made such an impression on Walt Disney that he modeled Sleeping Beauty's Castle in Disneyland after it.

staff and infrastructure for those seeking healing treatment. Today, there are hundreds of spa towns, thermal baths, and spa resorts. Perhaps the most famous is Baden-Baden. Its first bathing house was built in 1765.

NÜRNBERGER BRATWURST

There are approximately 1,500 different types of sausage, but there is only one Nürnberger bratwurst. The traditional Nürnberger bratwurst is a protected geographical indication under European Union (EU) law. This means that to be called a Nürnberger bratwurst a business must make it from pork loin with salt, pepper, marjoram, mace, and nutmeg. These bratwursts can contain maximum 35 percent fat, must be 2.75 to 3.5 inches (7–9 cm) long, and must weigh between 0.71 and 0.9 ounces (20 and 25 g).[14]

FOOD

For breakfast, many Germans eat whole wheat bread or buns with butter, jam, or local honey, along with sliced deli meats, cheese, and coffee or tea. Dinner is called *Abendbrot*, meaning "evening bread." It usually features whole wheat breads and deli meats and cheeses, but it might also include sausages, mustard, or pickles, to make a quick sandwich. There are approximately 1,500 varieties of German sausages.[13] Germans eat their main hot meal of the day at lunchtime, between noon and two o'clock. Traditionally, workers and children return home for this meal, but this has become more difficult to do in modern times. A typical German meal would include bratwurst or schnitzel—which is a breaded veal or pork cutlet—sauerkraut, and fried potatoes or spätzle, a German noodle or dumpling. In the northern region of the country, fish is a staple. It is customary

Considered the oldest fast-food joint in the world, the Sausage Kitchen in Regensburg opened in 1146 CE to serve boiled meat to workers building a nearby bridge.

to say "*Guten Appetit*," meaning "Enjoy your meal," before eating.

Along with their sausages, Germans enjoy their beer. Bavaria is home to the oldest brewery in the world. A former Benedictine monastery, the brewery dates to the year 1040 CE. The monks delivered their beer throughout Europe. Germany produces more than 7,000 varieties of beer.[15] And much like their bratwurst, Germans take their beer seriously. A law dating to 1516 says that German beer can contain only hops, malt (barley), yeast, and water. It can have no other ingredients. Over the course of 2020, Germans drank an average of 25 gallons (95 L) of beer per person.[16]

SPORTS

In Germany, soccer reigns supreme. It is popular to watch and play. There are thousands of amateur and semiprofessional soccer clubs across the country. There are also three tiers of professional leagues. The regional rivalries are fierce. Matches draw an average of 25,000 spectators.[17]

The German Olympic Sports Federation oversees amateur sport in Germany. It represents 89,000 clubs and 27 million members.[18] The German people also have abundant access to playing fields, gymnasiums, swimming pools, and training facilities. Going into the 2022 FIFA World Cup, Germany's men's national soccer team had won four men's FIFA World Cup titles, the second-most

Thomas Müller is a popular player from one of Germany's top teams, Bayern Munich. He has appeared in more than 100 international games.

wins behind Brazil. And heading into the 2023 FIFA Women's World Cup, the women's national soccer team was second in the number of Women's World Cup titles, with two wins. At that time, Germany was the only country that had won both men's and women's FIFA World Cups.

CHAPTER **SIX**

POLITICS

Germans have included social safety nets in German law since Otto von Bismarck first united the country. In the 1880s, the German government adopted social insurances to protect workers, including illness insurance, work-related accident insurance, and age and disability insurance. This was the beginning of Germany's welfare state. In 1919, the postwar Weimar Republic introduced Germany's first federal constitution. It included several provisions to guarantee the social welfare of the German people, becoming the first European constitution to include a detailed list of social rights. Hitler abolished the Weimer Constitution during his rule.

The Bundestag, Germany's lower legislative house, meets in the Reichstag.

Konrad Adenauer, chancellor of West Germany, signed the Basic Law on May 23, 1949.

THE BASIC LAW

After World War II, the Allies granted West Germany the right to form a federal republic. Eleven *Länder*, or "states," came together to form the *Bund*, or "federation." They established the capital of West Germany in the university town of Bonn. The communist regime of East Germany divided the five states that fell in its region into 15 *Bezirke*, or "administrative districts," with East Berlin as the capital.[1]

Germany's constitution, the *Grundgesetz*, or "Basic Law," went into effect on May 23, 1949. It was called the Basic Law because it was intended to be temporary until the reunification of Germany. West German ministers felt calling it a constitution and making it permanent would further alienate East Germany.

The overriding purpose of the Basic Law is respect of human dignity. The tone and content of the Basic Law reflects the human rights violations that occurred between 1933 and 1945 when Hitler and the Nazi Party were in power. No other criminal, asylum, or civil laws can conflict with the Basic Law. It is the dominant rule of order for the country and stands above all other rules and laws.

There are 146 articles in the Basic Law. The first 19 articles address fundamental rights.[2] These are human rights established by the government to protect people from injustices or violence from the state. These fundamental human rights apply to all people. They include freedom of faith, artistic expression, movement, association, marriage, and choice of occupation. These articles also guarantee equality before the law and the right to own property.

The Basic Law also includes several civil rights and social benefits that apply only to German citizens. Health care, unemployment and disability compensation, maternity and childcare provisions, education and job training, and pensions are all guaranteed under the Basic Law. Tax contributions from individuals and employers pay for the cost of these benefits. The Federal

In office 16 years, from 1982 to 1998, Helmut Kohl was the longest-serving chancellor of modern Germany.[4]

Constitutional Court assures compliance with the Basic Law. A two-thirds majority vote in both houses of parliament is required for any changes to be made to the Basic Law.[3]

When East and West Germany signed the Unification Treaty in 1990, they did not write a new constitution. Instead, East Germany agreed to join the Federal Republic of Germany, and the newly united Germany adopted the Basic Law as the constitution. Berlin again became the capital of Germany in 1991.

BRANCHES OF GOVERNMENT

All government powers are granted by the people through elections and referendums, which are votes the general public takes on single political questions. To avoid the centralized power that led to the Nazi Party's rise, the states have a lot of ability to self-govern. The Basic Law divides the powers and responsibilities of government between the federal government and states. The three most powerful positions in government are the federal president, the federal chancellor, and the president of the Bundestag.

Germany has three government branches: the executive, the legislative, and the judiciary. The Bundestag is the federal parliament. This is the legislative branch of government. The people elect

ANGELA MERKEL

Angela Merkel was the third chancellor of the reunited Federal Republic of Germany. Born in Hamburg in West Germany in 1954 but raised in East Germany, she pursued an education in physics. In 1986, she earned a doctorate in quantum chemistry.

After the Berlin Wall fell in 1989, Merkel joined the new Democratic Awakening party. In the first election post-reunification, Merkel won a seat in the Bundestag and became the minister of children and youth under Chancellor Helmut Kohl. She rose among the ranks quickly. In April 2000, the Christian Democratic Union elected Merkel head of its party. On November 22, 2005, at 51 years old, Merkel became chancellor. She was the first woman, first East German, and youngest person to hold the position. Her last full day in office was December 7, 2021.

Angela Merkel was the first woman and first non-Catholic to be head of the Christian Democratic Union.

members of the Bundestag every four years. The chief responsibilities of the Bundestag are to adopt new legislation and oversee federal government activities.

The Bundestag nominates the federal chancellor, who is the head of the executive branch and the head of government. The president of the Bundestag also holds the Federal Convention. This meeting typically happens every five years, and its purpose is to elect the federal president, who is head of state. All members of the Bundestag and representatives from all 16 states participate in this election.[5]

The federal president role is more ceremonial than that of the chancellor. The president is Germany's principal representative in international relations. In government, the president signs new legislation into law, grants pardons, and appoints federal judges, but this person can do none of these things without the additional signature of a minister or the chancellor.

The Bundesrat is the second legislative chamber of the German government. People do not vote for members of the Bundesrat directly. Instead, they vote for members of their state's parliament.

POLITICAL PARTIES

In 2021, there were seven political parties represented in Germany's federal election.[6] They were the Social Democratic Party (SPD), the Christian Democratic Union (CDU), the Christian Social Union (CSU), the Green Party, the Left Party, the Free Democratic Party (FDP), and the Alternative for Germany. The SPD was founded in 1875. It is Germany's oldest political party. It slightly edged out the incumbent CDU/CSU coalition, or alliance, to win the 2021 federal election. The SPD won by forming its own coalition with the Greens and FDP. SPD leader Olaf Scholz negotiated with his new partners for six weeks before the Bundestag swore him in as chancellor on December 8, 2021.

The Federal Constitutional Court is split into two groups of eight judges: the First Senate, *pictured*, and the Second Senate.

The members of the political party with the majority in a state's parliament make up the state government. The state government then selects some of its members to become part of the Bundesrat. The Bundesrat represents the voice of the individual states. The body plays mostly an advisory role in government. However, its approval is required to pass many laws, regulations, and constitutional amendments.

The judiciary branch is the third branch of government. The Bundesrat elects half of the 16 Federal Constitutional Court judges. The Bundestag elects the other half. The Federal Constitutional Court is responsible for ensuring judges apply national laws uniformly across all states and for upholding the constitutionality of government legislation and acts. Only the Federal

Constitutional Court can declare legislation unconstitutional. If a question of constitutionality comes up in a lower court case, the judge must suspend proceedings and send the question to the federal judges. There are also civil and criminal courts, as well as other special state-level courts.

CHURCH INFLUENCE

Germany does not have a national religion. However, Catholic and Protestant churches play a big role in public issues. The churches receive funds from both state and federal governments in Germany. The states pay the churches money in compensation for property losses dating back to the 1800s, when governments took away church property to give to German princes who had lost territory. The princes then paid the churches. Money has been going from the states to the churches ever since. Authorities estimate that states paid the equivalent of 20 billion euros (about $22.4 billion in US dollars) to churches between 1949 and 2019.[7]

Religious organizations also collect a membership fee through taxes. All registered Catholic and Protestant church members and

WEALTHY LANDOWNERS

The German Protestant and Catholic churches are wealthy landowners. Their total holdings are not known, but it is believed they own at least 3,200 square miles (8,300 square km) of German land between them. It is estimated that the Catholic Church has at least another 66,000 real estate holdings related to health care, education, and charitable work in Germany. The Protestant church is thought to have at least 50,000 holdings. There are 24,500 Catholic churches and 21,100 Protestant churches in Germany.[8]

Jewish community members pay this tax. The money ensures continuity of services the churches and Jewish communities provide. It funds building repairs, maintenance, and church staff. Citizens can opt out of paying the tax, but to do so, they must leave their church and give up any church services such as baptisms, weddings, or funerals. In 2019 alone, Catholic and Protestant churches received 12.7 billion euros (about $14.2 billion in US dollars) combined in church taxes.[9]

Although church leaders are not politicians, they do have a voice in policy. The churches have representatives on many supervisory boards, from conservation organizations to public broadcasting. The wealth of churches, their voices on supervisory boards, and the social services they provide, such as hospitals and daycares, give them a lot of influence.

FOREIGN RELATIONS

Germany recovered quickly in the decades following World War II. Less than 50 years after the war, many of the countries Germany fought, including Poland, Czechoslovakia, and France, became its partners in the European Union (EU). Other nations tend to view Germany favorably.

Germany's postwar foreign policy has focused on diplomacy and peace. The country entrenched human rights in the constitution, and these are a nonnegotiable issue in foreign policy. Germany's foreign policy fights for democracy and human rights, including for children, LGBTQ people, and women. It also promotes gender, religious, economic, and social rights. The country believes promoting these rights is not only the right thing to do but also in the best interest of global peace.

Germany is a trading nation surrounded by other European countries. It has developed strong economic and political partnerships with its neighbors. Membership in the EU is key to ensuring Germany has a voice in European foreign policy. The German government encourages close cooperation among EU nations. Safeguarding European borders, improving trust and security among the EU membership, and strengthening economic policies are the benefits of a strong EU that Germany promotes. Germany also has many international partnerships beyond Europe. The United States is a close ally, with strong economic and foreign policy ties to Germany.

The final cornerstone of Germany's foreign policy is peace. Germany is committed to global peace. It uses the frameworks of multinational organizations and partnerships, including the EU, North Atlantic Treaty Organization (NATO), and the G7 and G20 nations, to define its peace and security policies. NATO is a military alliance between many European and North American countries. The G7

THE EUROPEAN UNION

In 1993, Belgium, Denmark, France, Germany, Greece, Ireland, Italy, Luxembourg, the Netherlands, Portugal, Spain, and the United Kingdom formed the EU. The primary aim of the nations was to create a common currency. The EU created a new shared currency, the euro, in 2002. Foreign policy, border security, and justice were also common interests of the EU nations. Since 1993, more countries have joined the EU. The United Kingdom left the EU on January 31, 2020. In 2022, 19 of the 27 member nations used the euro as their currency.[10]

Berlin hosted a G7 meeting in May 2022. German leaders, including Federal Minister for Economic Cooperation and Development Svenja Schulze, spoke at the meeting.

nations are the seven countries with the largest and most advanced economies. The G20 is a geopolitical organization of the world's most advanced economies and the largest emerging economies. Germany's first course of action in any conflict is to find a diplomatic resolution. Seeking an end to nuclear weaponry is also a German foreign policy goal. Humanitarian aid is a pillar of its peace policy. Germany is one of the largest humanitarian aid donors worldwide.

CHAPTER **SEVEN**

ECONOMICS

In 1945, Germany was a nation devastated and divided by war. The country's industrial output was one-third its prewar production. Food production was half what it was before the war.[1] Food rationing was in place, and people had to barter because the German currency, the reichsmark, was worthless. More than four million Germans had died in the war.[2] Rebuilding seemed impossible.

But Germany completely reversed its economy. In 2020, its gross domestic product (GDP) stood at $4.1 trillion in US dollars.[3] Germany was the world's fourth-largest economy.[4]

After World War II, the Allied countries recognized that reviving the German economy would offset their costs of occupation. It was also clear that tensions

After World War I, Germany's central bank printed millions of banknotes to pay war reparations to other countries. This made the currency's value drop dramatically in 1922, so banks and people were left with large stacks of money that had become virtually worthless.

The Marshall Plan helped pay laborers in West Germany, including those laying streets.

between the Soviet Union and the United States were growing. It was in the interest of the United States to strengthen Germany and western Europe to defend against the Soviets and prevent the spread of communism across the continent.

THE ECONOMIC MIRACLE

The United States introduced the Marshall Plan, which focused on rehabilitating western Europe and stabilizing relationships between western European nations. Enacted in 1948, it was a four-year, $13 billion aid plan financed by the United States to rebuild cities, infrastructure, and industries across Europe. Initially, the United States offered aid to all countries, including the Soviet Union. The Soviets pulled out of the plan early. East Germany and several countries under Soviet control also pulled out. In the end, West Germany was among the nations that received aid.

France, which shares a border with Germany and suffered serious damage at the hands of the Germans, was not comfortable with Germany having industrial capabilities again. France, however, was desperate for the aid itself, so it came up with a solution. French foreign minister Robert Schuman presented the Schuman Declaration, which proposed that European nations pool coal and steel production. The declaration stated that merging these resources would make war between Germany and France "not merely unthinkable, but materially impossible." Schuman believed that merging the economic interests of European nations would elevate the standard of living for all. The Schuman Declaration opened the door to other alliances between western European nations.

Both the Marshall Plan and the Schuman Declaration helped kick-start Germany's recovery. But Ludwig Erhard became known as the father of the Wirtschaftswunder, or "economic miracle." Erhard, as Germany's economics minister, formulated a new German currency, the deutsche mark, to replace the worthless reichsmark. When West Germany issued the new currency on June 21, 1948, it reduced the amount available to individual Germans by 93 percent. This vastly decreased any remaining wealth Germans and corporations had, but it also gave them a currency that had value. This eliminated the need for bartering. Erhard also introduced large tax cuts to encourage spending and investments. Finally, he removed price controls and rationing that had been in place

In 1948, people in West Germany crowded exchange offices to swap the reichsmark with the new deutsche mark.

since the end of the war. Erhard's plan paid off for West Germany. The country's economy came alive quickly. Shopkeepers stocked their shelves with goods because people had money to pay for things. When the government first introduced the deutsche mark, West Germany's industrial production was 50 percent of what it was in 1936. Six months later, it had increased to 80 percent. Within a decade, its industrial production was four times greater.[5]

During the same time West Germany was experiencing a great recovery, East Germany struggled under communist rule and a command economy, meaning the government controlled production levels, prices, and wages. The weak economy was one thing that caused the citizen protests in East Germany that eventually led to the fall of the Berlin Wall and reunification. By the time Germany reunified, West Germany had one of the largest economies in the world.

LABOR FORCE AND EMPLOYMENT

In 2021, the services sector accounted for 69.8 percent of GDP. The industry sector accounted for 23.5 percent of GDP.[6] The overall unemployment rate was relatively low in 2021, with only 3.3 percent of willing workers unable to find a job.[7] It is a well-educated but aging workforce.

Germany has laws that require the government to care for its citizens. Support measures such as counseling, vocational training, and job placement are available to individuals who are out of work and for young people just starting out in the workforce. There is also a basic income support benefit for people who can work but cannot find jobs. The benefit helps people pay for basic needs such as housing and heating while they are not working.

Despite this social support, Germany still struggles with high rates of poverty and homelessness. In 2019, 15.9 percent of the population were at risk of poverty.[8] In 2020, it was reported that 2.8 million German children were growing up in poverty.[9] Homelessness is also on the rise. In 2022, an organization working to end homelessness estimated there were 860,000 homeless people in Germany; more than half were refugees.[10]

Like most Western nations, Germany is also facing increasing wealth inequality. The top 1 percent of wealthy Germans earn as much as the bottom 50 percent combined. The wealthiest 10 percent of German households own 65 percent of the country's assets.[11] It is one of the highest concentrations of wealth among countries belonging to the Organisation for Economic Co-operation and Development. This intergovernmental organization works to promote economic progress and world trade.

INDUSTRY AND RESOURCES

Some of the biggest names in automobiles, technology, and pharmaceuticals have come from Germany. The country is the world's fourth-largest producer of automobiles. It is also a country of innovation. Germans invented the automobile, the MP3 file format, the glue stick, and aspirin. In 2021, Germany ranked tenth among 132 economies on the World Economic Forum's Global Innovation Index.[12]

Germany's agricultural industry is a leader in the global food market. Farming is the country's fourth-largest industry.[13] Germany farms almost half of its land. The agricultural-food industry supports more than 275,000 companies and employs almost one million people.[14] The industry meets approximately 70 percent of domestic needs. Germany is the second-largest agricultural producer in Europe. The country exports one-third of its agricultural products. The leading crops grown are wheat, barley, and rye.[15]

ICONIC GERMAN AUTOMOTIVE COMPANIES

In 1876, Nikolaus Otto built the four-stroke internal combustion engine and launched Germany into the world of automotive manufacturing. By 1901, Germany was producing hundreds of vehicles a year. More than 120 years later, Germany manufactures some of the most luxurious and well-known automobile brands in the world. Audi, BMW, Porsche, Volkswagen, and Mercedes-Benz are all manufactured in Germany. Mercedes-Benz is the world's oldest car manufacturer.

IMPORTS AND EXPORTS

In 2021, Germany was the world's top exporter of vehicles, drugs and medicine, and auto parts and accessories. It was second in the world for exporting aircraft parts. Machinery and chemical products were among Germany's other top exports. In 2020, exported goods accounted for 43.4 percent of GDP.[16] Germany's top trading partners were China, the Netherlands, and the United States.

The German economy depends on having a reliable supply of raw materials both to support its own industries and to export to other countries. Germany has a strong mining industry and is self-sufficient for building materials such as sand and gravel. It is also a top producer of lignite coal, kaolin clay, rock salt, and potassium salt.

Merck, founded in 1668 in Germany, is the oldest pharmaceutical company in the world.[17]

Germany imports metals and energy. It has imported all its metal or recovered it from scrap since 1992, when the last metal ore mine shut down. It is also heavily dependent on imported natural gas and crude oil.

INFRASTRUCTURE AND TRANSPORTATION

Germany's location in the heart of Europe makes it a vital transportation hub. It has an extensive network of railways, waterways, seaports, airports, and highways. Hamburg is a key port city,

Germany has a robust railway network run by Deutsche Bahn, along with train connections to several countries. In 2019, Deutsche Bahn carried 2.6 billion passengers.

with nine million containers passing through each year.[18] There are also hundreds of airports in Germany. Frankfurt am Main Airport is its busiest, with 24.8 million passengers using it in 2021.[19]

Germany is also home to the autobahn. The autobahn was the world's first motorway. It was originally a stretch of highway just a few miles long for racing. When Hitler came to power in the 1930s, he saw the advantage in having a high-speed roadway and began construction of two highways: one running east to west, the other north to south. By the time construction came to a halt during the war, workers had completed 1,322 miles (2,128 km). After the war, the new West German government invested heavily in extending the highway system. The autobahn is now more than 8,000 miles (12,800 km) long.[20] It is also a destination for speed lovers because there is no speed limit on some parts of the autobahn.

HAMBURG

The densely built urban areas in Hamburg are UNESCO World Heritage sites. Speicherstadt in Hamburg is one of the largest unified historic port warehouse complexes in the world. It was built on a group of narrow islands in the Elbe River in 1885. Speicherstadt is called the city of warehouses. Developers have kept the historical character of the 15 large warehouse blocks but have technologically upgraded all the buildings. The heritage site also includes a network of secondary buildings, streets, canals, and bridges. The neighboring Kontorhaus District was developed between the 1920s and 1940s to house port-related businesses.

TOURISM

Germany is home to 46 UNESCO World Heritage sites and 15 UNESCO biosphere reserves. These, combined with its northern beaches, vast vineyards, and lush forests, make Germany an increasingly attractive tourist destination. Between 1990 and 2019, the number of foreign visitors

The Black Forest's hills, valleys, forests, meadows, lakes, and waterfalls attract local and international tourists alike.

GERMAN IS EASY FOR ENGLISH SPEAKERS

German is one of the easiest languages for English speakers to learn. English is a Germanic language. The German alphabet uses the same letters as the English alphabet. Three vowels, *ä*, *ö*, and *ü*, also use marks called umlauts. An umlaut is two dots above the vowels to indicate a change in sound. Germans also use an *Eszett*, symbolized as ß. This character is unique to German. It makes the sound of the letters *s* and *z* combined. Eighty of the 100 most used words in English originate from German.[23] Some English and German words, such as arm, kindergarten, and hand, are the same.

to Germany annually rose from 34.4 million to 89.9 million.[21] It is a popular destination, especially for other Europeans.

Germany's robust economy, diverse trade relationships, and innovative industries also make it the leading business travel destination in Europe and the number one European location for international trade fairs and conferences. In 2019, the travel and tourism industry accounted for 9.8 percent of GDP, and it employed 5.9 million people. The industry suffered deep losses during the COVID-19 pandemic, which began in 2020. Its contribution to GDP dropped to 5.5 percent in 2020. More than 440,000 people lost their jobs.[22]

CHAPTER **EIGHT**

GERMANY TODAY

Germany is a country that has overcome great adversity to rise to a position of global leadership. Since West Germany gained its sovereignty in 1955, and even more so since unification in 1990, government leaders have put human rights and social welfare at the forefront of their policies. Germany remains an important nation globally today.

FAMILY LIFE

There are more than eight million families with children living in Germany. Most of these include married couples consisting of a man and a woman, but in 2019

Most German parents have one or two children.

there were also 1.5 million single parents, 8.2 million unmarried couples, and 52,000 same-sex couples in the country with children.[1] Most families have just one or two children. Germans are waiting to have children until they are older, with many being over 30 when they have their first babies. In families, 92.9 percent of fathers and 74.7 percent of mothers work at least part-time.[2] In 2019, 94 percent of children ages three to five were enrolled in some form of preschool or childcare.[3]

Teenagers watch television, surf the internet, listen to music, and hang out with friends. Parents typically give teens a lot of freedom and expect their kids to take care of their own affairs and to be independent. It is uncommon for teenagers to own cars. Walking, cycling, or taking public transit are the preferred methods of transportation.

Germans of all ages value the outdoors. The annual festival Oktoberfest is famous for its outdoor beer gardens. Germans also hold Christmas markets outside in the cold through December. In winter, parents bundle up children and send them outside to play as soon as they can walk. Hiking is the most

OKTOBERFEST

The first Oktoberfest, held in 1810, was little like the modern-day version of the celebration. It was a five-day event held to commemorate the marriage of the crown prince of Bavaria, who became King Louis I. It ended with a horse race. The people of Munich enjoyed the event so much it became an annual affair. It lasts for two weeks, ending on the first Sunday in October. Over time, organizers added booths serving food and drinks, and breweries started setting up large tents with live music. Oktoberfest has grown to be the largest folk festival in the world. Each year the city of Munich welcomes more than six million people who consume more than two million gallons (7.6 million L) of beer during the festival.[4]

popular outdoor activity. Germany has an extensive network of hiking trails that are enjoyed by most of the population.

SCHULTÜTE

A *Schultüte* is a paper cone filled with gifts that children get on the day they begin school. The tradition dates to the 1700s. Originally, the cones were once wrapped in simple paper, but over time, they have become elaborate. Parents usually fill them with candy, small toys, and school supplies. The tradition has extended to sometimes giving schultüte to young adults who are starting their first day of technical college or university.

EDUCATIONAL OPTIONS

Germans value education. Children are required by law to attend school from ages six to 15.[5] All public education is free, including university. German children begin *Grundschule*, or "elementary school," in grade one at age six. The first day of school is a special day for German children. It is a day of transition that is celebrated by families. Children get *Schultüte*, paper cones filled with gifts and treats. Elementary school goes from grade one to grade four. Before children move on to secondary school, parents and teachers decide on the type of school they will attend.

There are three options: *Hauptschule, Realschule,* and *Gymnasium*. Those who choose Hauptschule, the lowest tier secondary school, attend for five years. When students graduate in grade ten, they usually go on to vocational training. Students who choose Realschule, a technical

Students prepare to take an exam to gain entry into a post-secondary institute.

academic high school, also attend for five years. Upon graduation from Realschule, students qualify for higher education at a technical college. Graduating from Realschule is also a prerequisite for business administration careers. Students who want to qualify for university choose Gymnasium, a college preparatory high school, that runs from grade five to grade 12 or 13.

Many German students go to a Gymnasium. These students must pass exams to get their Abitur, similar to a high school diploma. The Abitur guarantees students a place in a German post-secondary institute but not in a field of study. Some popular fields have limited seats, so students must have backup options. In the 2020 to 2021 winter semester, there were almost three million students enrolled in Germany's 422 institutions of higher education.[6]

Some Syrian refugees trained to become train drivers in Germany.

RECENT CHALLENGES

The early 2000s brought new challenges to Germany. In 2015, refugees of war and terrorism from Syria, Afghanistan, and Iraq began arriving to the European continent. It was a humanitarian tragedy. German chancellor Angela Merkel stepped up and said Germany would accept one million refugees that year, famously stating, “We can manage it.”[7] By the end of 2020, more

A researcher from Charité hospital studies the new coronavirus in January 2020.

than 1.1 million refugees were living in Germany.[8] Approximately half the refugees had found a job, paid training, or an internship.

Employment rates for the refugees were still far lower than for the rest of the German population. In 2018, a much larger percentage declared they had good or very good German language skills compared to those just arriving in the country. Public support for migrant populations was divided, with a small majority approving and others disapproving. The bureaucratic processing systems were overwhelmed, and many of the refugees found it difficult to integrate into German society.

In 2020, the COVID-19 pandemic spread across the globe. Germany took a four-pronged approach to fighting the deadly virus: prevent, detect, contain, and treat. One of the first COVID-19 diagnostic tests was developed in Charité hospital in Berlin, and the country fast-tracked access to testing. It had success containing the spread of the virus in senior homes during the first wave. And the country had plenty of hospital beds, so its intensive care units were not overwhelmed. This kept both the rate of infection and the death rate under control for a time. But starting in October 2020, cases began to surge.

German biotech firm BioNTech, in partnership with US pharmaceutical company Pfizer, developed the first COVID-19 vaccine. By March 2022, 76 percent of the German population was vaccinated.[9] Germany also distributed the vaccine globally. Between August 2021 and March 2022, it donated vaccine doses to be distributed to developing countries. It also assisted many countries by sending relief packages that included ventilators, medical equipment, and masks.

Thousands of Ukrainians came to Germany, where the government, organizations, and individual volunteers worked to provide for the new arrivals.

Germany faced a new challenge in 2022. Since the end of World War II, Germany has been a pacifist nation. It has limited its military spending. Germany has also worked to have positive diplomatic relations with Russia. On February 24, 2022, Russia invaded Ukraine. Russia's invasion brought war far too close to Germany's borders. On February 27, 2022, in an emergency session of parliament, Chancellor Olaf Scholz announced a budget of 100 billion euros ($113 billion in US dollars) for the German army.[10] It was a stunning change in policy. The foreign minister also announced Germany would send weapons to Ukraine. By March 16, 2022, approximately 147,000 Ukrainians fleeing war registered as refugees in Germany.[11]

Another pressing challenge is climate change. Germany has experienced extreme heat waves, and in 2021, flash floods killed nearly 200 people.[12] With global temperatures rising, scientists expect things to get worse. Germany is committed to combating climate change. In 2016, the federal cabinet adopted the Climate Action Plan 2050. The plan's goal centers on the country achieving greenhouse gas neutrality, meaning it removes as much greenhouse gas from the atmosphere as it emits, by 2045. In 2021, Germany's goal was to reduce emissions by at least 65 percent by 2030 and by at least 88 percent by 2040.[13]

The Bundeswehr, the German armed forces, is restricted to 370,000 personnel.[14]

FATAL FLOODS

In July 2021, the worst natural disaster to hit Germany in decades flooded vast areas of river valleys. Rain flooded parts of the country with 39 gallons (148 L) of rain per square meter in 48 hours. In the most extreme case, six inches (15.4 cm) of rain fell in 24 hours at the Köln-Stammheim station, shattering the old record of 3.7 inches (9.5 cm).[15] In the town of Altenahr, floodwaters washed away bridges and destroyed homes. Three months later, reconstruction still had not begun.

Germany has maintained a stable global presence for 75 years. Its dramatic recovery after World War II demonstrated the power of the democratic system. It uses diplomacy and encourages dialogue in conflicts. By welcoming refugees, donating vaccines, and acting on climate change, it sets humanitarian examples. Germany is an innovative, hardworking nation that continues to have global influence today.

ESSENTIAL **FACTS**

OFFICIAL NAME: FEDERAL REPUBLIC OF GERMANY

GEOGRAPHY

Area: 137,847 square miles (357,022 sq km)

Highest Elevation: Zugspitze at 9,721 feet (2,963 m)

Lowest Elevation: Neuendorf-Sachsenbande at –11.5 feet (–3.5 m)

PEOPLE

Population: 84.3 million (2022 est.)

Most Populous City: Berlin (3.6 million)

Ethnic Groups: Mainly German, but also Turkish, Polish, Syrian, Romanian, and other

Religions: Christianity (Roman Catholicism, Protestantism), Islam, other, none

GOVERNMENT

Type of Government: Federal parliamentary republic

Capital: Berlin

Head of State: President

Head of Government: Chancellor

Legislature: Bicameral, with a Bundesrat and a Bundestag

ECONOMY

Currency: Euro

Major Industries: Automobiles, chemicals, pharmaceuticals, food and beverages, machinery

Natural Resources: Lignite, salt, construction materials such as sand and gravel, timber, farmable land

NATIONAL SYMBOLS

National Anthem: "Das Lied der Deutschen" ("Song of the Germans")

National Coat of Arms: Black eagle with red beak and feet on a golden background

National Motto: "Einigkeit und Recht und Freiheit" ("Unity and Justice and Freedom")

GLOSSARY

ARCHIPELAGO
A group of islands, or a stretch of sea containing many islands.

COALITION
A collection of groups or people that have joined together for a common purpose.

COMMUNISM
A political system in which the government controls the economy and owns all property.

CONCENTRATION CAMP
A place where prisoners of war, political prisoners, or refugees are held in poor conditions and are forced to work.

ESTUARY
An area where river water meets seawater.

FERMENTED
Chemically changed, often with the involvement of yeast or microorganisms, in a way that results in the production of alcohol.

FJORD
A long, deep, and narrow sea inlet sitting between very high cliffs.

GROSS DOMESTIC PRODUCT (GDP)
The monetary value of all final goods and services produced within a nation's geographic borders over a specified period of time.

LGBTQ
An acronym referring to lesbian, gay, bisexual, transgender, and queer or questioning people.

MEDIAN
A value in a set of data that has an equal number of data points above and below it.

MYCOLOGICAL
Having to do with the study of fungi.

SOVEREIGNTY
The power of a state or group to govern itself.

TOPOGRAPHY
The arrangement of physical features of a landscape, including mountains, hills, and rivers.

ADDITIONAL **RESOURCES**

SELECTED BIBLIOGRAPHY

Federal Ministry of Food and Agriculture. *The Forests of Germany: Selected Results of the Third National Forest Inventory*. BMEL, Bonn, October 2014.

"Interesting Facts about Germany." *German National Tourist Board*, n.d., germany.travel. Accessed 25 Apr. 2022.

"Reichstag in Berlin." *Visit Berlin*, n.d., visitberlin.de. Accessed 25 Apr. 2022.

FURTHER READINGS

Edwards, Sue Bradford. *Russia*. Abdo, 2023.

Hamen, Susan E. *Fighting COVID-19 Abroad*. Abdo, 2023.

Sheen, Barbara. *Growing Up in Germany*. ReferencePoint, 2017.

ONLINE RESOURCES

To learn more about Germany, please visit **abdobooklinks.com** or scan this QR code. These links are routinely monitored and updated to provide the most current information available.

MORE INFORMATION

For more information on this subject, contact or visit the following organizations:

Deutscher Bundestag (German Bundestag)
Platz der Republik 1
11011 Berlin
bundestag.de/en
The Bundestag is home to the Parliament of the Federal Government of Germany. Its seat is in the Reichstag in Berlin. Members of the Bundestag oversee legislative processes and scrutinize government work.

Deutsches Historisches Museum (German Historical Museum)
Unter den Linden 2
10117 Berlin
info@dhm.de
dhm.de/en/
The Deutsches Historisches Museum in Berlin is Germany's national history museum. It has more than one million objects in its collection and a public reference library with old and valuable prints and photos.

SOURCE **NOTES**

CHAPTER 1. A TOUR OF GERMANY

1. Jan Conway. "Number of Active Beer Breweries in Germany from 2008 to 2020." *Statista*, 18 Mar. 2022, statista.com. Accessed 1 July 2022.
2. "Tiergarten." *Encyclopedia Britannica*, 27 Mar. 2009, britannica.com. Accessed 1 July 2022.
3. "Memorial to the Murdered Jews of Europe." *Visit Berlin*, n.d., visitberlin.de. Accessed 1 July 2022.
4. "Brandenburg Gate." *Encyclopedia Britannica*, 14 Apr. 2014, britannica.com. Accessed 1 July 2022.
5. "Unter den Linden." *Visit Berlin*, n.d., visitberlin.de. Accessed 1 July 2022.
6. "Berlin Wall." *Encyclopedia Britannica*, 10 July 2020, britannica.com. Accessed 1 July 2022.
7. "Berlin Wall: Victims of the Wall." *Berlin*, n.d., berlin.de. Accessed 1 July 2022.
8. "Thousands of Museums, Millions of Visits." *Deutschland.de*, 28 Jan. 2022, deutschland.de. Accessed 1 July 2022.

CHAPTER 2. GEOGRAPHY

1. "Germany." *CIA World Factbook*, 27 June 2022, cia.gov. Accessed 1 July 2022.
2. "Wadden Sea." *UNESCO World Heritage Convention*, n.d., whc.unesco.org. Accessed 1 July 2022.
3. "Upper Middle Rhine Valley." *UNESCO World Heritage Convention*, n.d., whc.unesco.org. Accessed 1 July 2022.
4. Benjamin Elisha Sawe. "Major Rivers of Germany." *World Atlas*, 25 Apr. 2017, worldatlas.com. Accessed 1 July 2022.
5. "Wine Map of Germany." *Vineyards.com*, n.d., vineyards.com. Accessed 1 July 2022.
6. "Geography of Germany." *World Facts US*, n.d., worldfacts.us. Accessed 1 July 2022.
7. "Geography of Germany," *World Facts US*.
8. "Black Forest." *Encyclopedia Britannica*, 12 Aug. 2019, britannica.com. Accessed 5 July 2022.
9. "Germany," *CIA World Factbook*.
10. Peter John Heather, et al. "Germany." *Encyclopedia Britannica*, 29 June 2022, britannica.com. Accessed 5 July 2022.
11. "Sunshine in Germany." *Ru-Geld.de*, n.d., ru-geld.de. Accessed 6 July 2022.
12. George McDonald. "Regions in Brief in the Fairy Tale Road." *Frommer's*, n.d., frommers.com. Accessed 5 July 2022.
13. "Germany at a Glance." *Facts about Germany*, n.d., tatsachen-ueber-deutschland.de. Accessed 5 July 2022.
14. "Population of Cities in Germany (2022)." *World Population Review*, n.d., worldpopulationreview.com. Accessed 5 July 2022.
15. "Population Density (People per Sq. Km of Land Area)—European Union." *World Bank*, n.d., data.worldbank.org. Accessed 5 July 2022.

CHAPTER 3. PLANTS AND ANIMALS

1. Kim Berg. "9 Facts about Species Protection." *Deutschland.de*, 30 Apr. 2021, deutschland.de. Accessed 5 July 2022.
2. Berg, "9 Facts about Species Protection," *Deutschland.de*.
3. Kay-Alexander Scholz. "Wolves and Livestock: Can They Live in Harmony in Germany?" *DW*, 4 Apr. 2021, dw.com. Accessed 5 July 2022.
4. "Salmon, Danube." *Encyclopedia.com*, 21 June 2022, encyclopedia.com. Accessed 5 July 2022.
5. "Wieviele Pilzarten gibt es? [How Many Types of Mushrooms Are There?]." *Deutsche Gesellschaft für Mykologie e.V.*, n.d., dgfm-ev.de. Accessed 5 July 2022.
6. "Vögel Deutschlands [Birds of Germany]." *Club300*, n.d., club300.de. Accessed 5 July 2022.
7. Berg, "9 Facts about Species Protection," *Deutschland.de*.
8. "Forests in Germany." *Federal Ministry of Food and Agriculture*, n.d., bmel.de. Accessed 20 July 2022.
9. "Black Forest." *Encyclopedia Britannica*, 12 Aug. 2019, britannica.com. Accessed 5 July 2022.

10. Victor Kiprop. "The National Parks of Germany." *World Atlas*, 24 July 2017, worldatlas.com. Accessed 5 July 2022.

11. "Checking Management Efficiency: Evaluation of German National Parks." *Nationale Naturlandschaften*, n.d., nationale-naturlandschaften.de. Accessed 5 July 2022.

12. "Checking Management Efficiency," *Nationale Naturlandschaften*.

13. "Urban Green Spaces." *Federal Ministry of the Interior and Community*, n.d., bmi.bund.de. Accessed 5 July 2022.

14. "Green Berlin." *Sustain Europe*, 22 Apr. 2019, sustaineurope.com. Accessed 20 July 2022.

CHAPTER 4. HISTORY

1. "German Confederation." *Encyclopedia Britannica*, 16 Jan. 2012, britannica.com. Accessed 5 July 2022.

2. "Explore WWII History." *The National WWII Museum*, n.d., nationalww2museum.org. Accessed 5 July 2022.

3. John Graham Royde-Smith and Thomas A. Hughes. "World War II." *Encyclopedia Britannica*, 28 Feb. 2022, britannica.com. Accessed 5 July 2022.

4. "The Holocaust." *The National WWII Museum*, n.d., nationalww2museum.org. Accessed 5 July 2022.

5. "Holocaust Misconceptions." *Illinois Holocaust Museum & Education Center*, n.d., ilholocaustmuseum.org. Accessed 5 July 2022.

6. "Research Starters: Worldwide Deaths in World War II." *The National WWII Museum*, n.d., nationalww2museum.org. Accessed 5 July 2022.

CHAPTER 5. PEOPLE AND CULTURE

1. D. Clark. "Estimated Population of European Countries in 2021." *Statista*, 21 July 2021, statista.com. Accessed 5 July 2022.

2. "Germany." *CIA World Factbook*, 27 June 2022, cia.gov. Accessed 5 July 2022.

3. "Birth Rate, Crude (per 1,000 People)—Germany." *World Bank*, n.d., data.worldbank.org. Accessed 5 July 2022.

4. "No Population Growth Expected for 2021." *Statistisches Bundesamt*, 20 Jan. 2022, destatis.de. Accessed 5 July 2022.

5. "Life Expectancy of the World Population." *Worldometer*, n.d., worldometers.info. Accessed 5 July 2022.

6. "Germany," *CIA World Factbook*.

7. Oishimaya Sen Nag. "What Languages Are Spoken in Germany?" *World Atlas*, 13 June 2018, worldatlas.com. Accessed 5 July 2022.

8. Sen Nag, "What Languages Are Spoken?" *World Atlas*.

9. "Germany," *CIA World Factbook*.

10. Kathleen Schuster. "Catholic and Protestant Influence in Germany." *DW*, 1 Apr. 2021, dw.com. Accessed 5 July 2022.

11. Vera Schnepp. "Why Are There So Many Castles in Germany?" *History of Yesterday*, 11 Feb. 2021, historyofyesterday.com. Accessed 5 July 2022.

12. "Neuschwanstein Castle." *Encyclopedia Britannica*, 11 Oct. 2019, britannica.com. Accessed 5 July 2022.

13. Erin Porter. "Germany's Best Sausages." *TripSavvy*, 12 Mar. 2020, tripsavvy.com. Accessed 5 July 2022.

14. Kae Lani Palmisano. "Here's Why Nuremberg's Bratwursts Are Protected by EU Law." *USA Today 10Best*, 24 Apr. 2018, 10best.com. Accessed 5 July 2022.

15. "Guide to German Beer." *GermanFoods*, n.d., germanfoods.org. Accessed 5 July 2022.

16. "Per Capita Consumption of Beer in Germany from 1950 to 2021." *Statista*, 7 June 2022, statista.com. Accessed 5 July 2022.

17. "Sports in Germany." *The German Way*, n.d., german-way.com. Accessed 5 July 2022.

18. "Sports in Germany," *The German Way*.

SOURCE **NOTES** CONTINUED

CHAPTER 6. POLITICS

1. Peter John Heather, et al. "Germany." *Encyclopedia Britannica*, 29 June 2022, britannica.com. Accessed 5 July 2022.
2. "Basic Law." *Deutscher Bundestag*, 29 Sept. 2020, btg-bestellservice.de. Accessed 5 July 2022.
3. "Germany's Most Important Book." *Deutschland.de*, 17 Apr. 2019, deutschland.de. Accessed 5 July 2022.
4. "Helmut Kohl." *Encyclopedia Britannica*, 12 June 2022, britannica.com. Accessed 5 July 2022.
5. "Federal States of Germany." *Deutschland.de*, 18 May 2022, deutschland.de. Accessed 5 July 2022.
6. Rina Goldenberg. "Germany's Political Parties—What You Need to Know" *DW*, 5 Oct. 2021, dw.com. Accessed 5 July 2022.
7. Tom Heneghan. "Germany Continues Payments to Churches." *Religion News*, 13 Feb. 2019, religionnews.com. Accessed 5 July 2022.
8. Kathleen Schuster. "Catholic and Protestant Influence in Germany." *DW*, 1 Apr. 2021, dw.com. Accessed 5 July 2022.
9. Schuster, "Catholic and Protestant Influence," *DW*.
10. "Countries in the EU and EEA." *Gov.uk*, n.d., gov.uk. Accessed 5 July 2022.

CHAPTER 7. ECONOMICS

1. David R. Henderson. "German Economic Miracle." *Econlib*, n.d., econlib.org. Accessed 9 Aug. 2022.
2. John Graham Royde-Smith and Thomas A. Hughes. "World War II." *Encyclopedia Britannica*, 28 Feb. 2022, britannica.com. Accessed 11 July 2022.
3. Aaron O'Neill. "Germany: GDP from 2010 to 2021." *Statista*, 9 May 2022, statista.com. Accessed 5 July 2022.
4. Caleb Silver. "The Top 25 Economies in the World." *Investopedia*, 27 June 2022, investopedia.com. Accessed 5 July 2022.
5. Gregory Gethard. "The German Economic Miracle." *Investopedia*, 29 June 2021, investopedia.com. Accessed 5 July 2022.
6. Aaron O'Neill. "Germany: Share of Economic Sectors in GDP." *Statista*, 23 Mar. 2022, statista.com. Accessed 5 July 2022.
7. "German Labour Market to Year 2011, 2020 and 2021." *Statistisches Bundesamt*, 22 June 2022, destatis.de. Accessed 5 July 2022.
8. "Poverty Watch Report 2021: EAPN Germany." *European Anti-Poverty Network*, 2021, eapn.eu. Accessed 5 July 2022.
9. "1 in 5 Children in Germany Grow Up in Poverty." *DW*, 22 July 2020, dw.com. Accessed 5 July 2022.
10. "Global Homelessness Statistics." *Homeless World Cup*, n.d., homelessworldcup.org. Accessed 5 July 2022.
11. "Inequalities in Germany." *Make Europe Sustainable for All*, n.d., sdgwatcheurope.org. Accessed 5 July 2022.
12. "Germany." *Global Innovation Index 2021*, 2021, wipo.int. Accessed 5 July 2022.
13. O'Neill, "Germany: Share of Economic Sectors," *Statista*.
14. *Understanding Farming: Facts and Figures about German Farming.* BMEL, November 2020, bmel.de. Accessed 5 July 2022.
15. "Europe's Second-Largest Agricultural Producer." *Miller Magazine*, 12 Dec. 2019, millermagazine.com. Accessed 5 July 2022.
16. "Exports of Goods and Services (% of GDP)—Germany." *World Bank*, n.d., data.worldbank.org. Accessed 5 July 2022.
17. Dagmar Zindel. "Merck, the Oldest Pharma Company Turns 350." *DW*, 16 July 2018, dw.com. Accessed 5 July 2022.
18. "Adjustment of the Navigation Channel on the Elbe." *Port of Hamburg*, n.d., hafen-hamburg.de. Accessed 5 July 2022.
19. Evgenia Koptyug. "Leading Airports in Germany." *Statista*, 17 Mar. 2022, statista.com. Accessed 5 July 2022.
20. Marcel Krueger. "How German Autobahns Changed the World." *CNN Travel*, 23 Dec. 2021, cnn.com. Accessed 5 July 2022.
21. "Destination Germany Provides an Attractive Setting for Successful Business." *German Convention Bureau*, n.d., gcb.de. Accessed 5 July 2022.
22. "WTTC Research Reveals Travel & Tourism Sector's Contribution to Germany's GDP Dropped a Staggering €161 Billion in 2020." *World Travel & Tourism Council*, 8 Apr. 2021, wttc.org. Accessed 5 July 2022.
23. "English Is a Germanic Language." *Rosetta Stone*, n.d., rosettastone.com. Accessed 5 July 2022.

CHAPTER 8. GERMANY TODAY

1. "Diverse Living Arrangements." *Facts about Germany*, n.d., tatsachen-ueber-deutschland.de. Accessed 21 July 2022.

2. "Three in Four Mothers in Germany Were in Employment in 2019." *Statistisches Bundesamt*, 5 Mar. 2021, destatis.de. Accessed 21 July 2022.

3. "Germany: Highlights." *OECD iLibrary*, 2021, oecd-ilibrary.org. Accessed 7 July 2022.

4. "The History of Oktoberfest." *Oktoberfest.de*, n.d., oktoberfest.de. Accessed 5 July 2022.

5. Martina Schüttler-Hansper. "This Is How the German School System Works." *Deutschland.de*, 11 July, 2019, deutschland.de. Accessed 5 July 2022.

6. "The Right University." *Deutscher Akademischer Austauschdienst*, n.d., daad.de. Accessed 5 July 2022.

7. Nette Nöstlinger. "Revisiting Merkel's Refugee Pledge." *Politico*, 7 Dec. 2021, politico.eu. Accessed 5 July 2022.

8. "Germany Fact Sheet." *UNHCR*, 11 Mar. 2021, unhcr.org. Accessed 5 July 2022.

9. Hannah Ritchie, et al. "COVID-19 Vaccinations." *Our World in Data*, 5 July 2022, ourworldindata.org. Accessed 5 July 2022.

10. Natasha Turak. "Germany Announces Major Defense Policy Shift." *CNBC*, 27 Feb. 2022, cnbc.com. Accessed 5 July 2022.

11. "About 150,000 Ukrainian Refugees Have Arrived in Germany So Far." *Schengen Visa*, 16 Mar. 2022, schengenvisainfo.com. Accessed 5 July 2022.

12. "Fatal Floods Expose Gaps in Germany's Disaster Preparedness." *Climate Home News*, 20 July 2021, climatechangenews.com. Accessed 5 July 2022.

13. "Immediate Climate Action Programme for 2022." *Federal Ministry of Finance*, 23 June 2021, bundesfinanzministerium.de. Accessed 5 July 2022.

14. "The History of the German Army." *Bundeswehr*, n.d., bundeswehr.de. Accessed 5 July 2022.

15. Jonathan Watts. "Climate Scientists Shocked by Scale of Floods in Germany." *Guardian*, 16 July 2021, theguardian.com. Accessed 5 July 2022.

INDEX

ABOUT THE **AUTHOR**

RACQUEL FORAN

Racquel Foran is a freelance writer from Coquitlam, British Columbia, Canada. She has authored several nonfiction titles for school-age readers covering diverse subjects such as organ transplants, autism, and North Korea, among others. When she is not writing, she enjoys tending to her Little Free Library, painting, and hiking by the river with her dogs.